'Sitting oppos[...]
you your child[...]
illness, conditi[...]
disability is ne[...]
moments will live with us for the rest of
our lives, defining us and changing the
landscape of our families forever.'

Yvonne Newbold,
The Special Parent's Handbook

The 'ten rules' concept sets out to be gently provocative. Sadly, the 'rules' in this booklet are reflective of many of the practices we have come across that cause so many problems for people with learning disabilities who are on the autism spectrum, and those who care for and support them, making it very difficult for them to access the quality of healthcare the rest of us take for granted.

We hope it will be a useful starting point for discussion and a catalyst for action.

About the authors

Viki Ainsworth is a journalist, copywriter and director of a media training and TV talent agency. She is also an expert by lived experience and is on parental advisory panels for Great Ormond Street Hospital and NHS England. Viki has a BSc (Econ) in International Relations, a Postgraduate Diploma in Journalism and a Postgraduate Diploma in Philosophy, and she is also an Applied Behavioural Analysis therapist.

Jim Blair is currently a Consultant Nurse Intellectual (Learning) Disabilities at Great Ormond Street Hospital, Associate Professor Intellectual (Learning) Disabilities at Kingston University and St Georges' University of London as well as Clinical Advisor Learning Disabilities NHS England. He is also the Health Advisor at the British Institute of Learning Disabilities and the Learning Disability Advisor to the Sates of Jersey and Guernsey. From 2011-2013, Jim was Vice Chairman of Special Olympics Great Britain. Jim is an Expert Advisor to the Parliamentary Health Service Ombudsman, an advisor for the Down Syndrome Medical Interest Group and is on the editorial board of www.intellectualdisability.info. Jim is also a Specialist Clinical Advisor to the Care Quality Commission.

Introduction

A diagnosis of learning disabilities and/or autism can happen at any point in an individual's life, with some being diagnosed very young and others not receiving a diagnosis until later in life. Receiving such a diagnosis should bring freedom – freedom from worrying what, if anything, is wrong; freedom from wondering; freedom to move forward with all the information needed to live a fulfilling and rewarding life. Sadly, too often it means the opposite, and people diagnosed with a learning disability and/or autism often find the doors to a fulfilling life shutting in front of them.

Perceived societal 'norms' perpetuate the stigma surrounding those who develop differently, and this can cause considerable dismay when a diagnosis is received, especially when that diagnosis is delivered badly. The way in which a diagnosis is delivered is often so without thought or preparation that it consequently ensures lasting emotional trauma to the individuals involved and their loved ones. Herein lies the purpose of this booklet.

With this booklet we aim to challenge directly the method and moment a diagnosis is given, and to help medical professionals seize upon it as the defining opportunity to set individuals and their families off on a positive and hopeful path, rather than on a negative, diminished one. We aim to educate all those involved in the journey leading to a diagnosis and subsequent care and support. Only through education can we push back the boundaries that often come with a diagnosis, and even aim to abolish them altogether, in order to ensure inclusivity, acceptance and access to a fulfilling life for all individuals with learning disabilities and those on the autism spectrum.

Make sure you tell us, 'I'm afraid it's bad news...'

☢ Reinforce my fears that disability is a bad thing and something to be ashamed of.

☢ Anything less than perfectly 'normal' has to be 'bad'.

Positive practises

Positive practice

☺ Don't use judgmental language – 'I'm afraid', 'unfortunately' and 'bad' are words loaded with negativity... Avoid them!

☺ You may not be able to imagine living with the consequences of a particular diagnosis, but the individuals and families will have to. Make sure you give them the mental space to deal with it in as positive a way as possible.

☺ You don't have to pretend it's good news, nor do you have to emphasise that it's bad news, just keep it neutral and deliver the necessary information with support ready for the family as necessary.

Just drop that diagnosis bombshell

☢ Just throw it in at the end of a rushed conversation.

☢ Maybe do it in a busy public area for maximum traumatic impact?

☢ A body blow is always most effective when you don't see it coming.

Positive practice

☺ Delivering test results may be part of your work routine, but receiving them is definitely *not* routine for the individual and their families.

☺ Give some thought to how you might deliver each diagnosis. It's worth preparing the best way to deliver the diagnosis in each instance to reduce emotional trauma.

☺ Find somewhere calm and private before delivering diagnosis news.

☺ People with learning disabilities and those on the autism spectrum, along with their families, will react in different ways – they deserve a quiet space to process information.

☺ Give people time to digest the news properly and to ask any initial questions they might have.

Rule 3

Ensure that the first we know of a diagnosis is in a letter

☢ Surely we've guessed by now anyway?

☢ Someone must have told us already, it's so obvious.

Positive practice

☺ A diagnosis is often incredibly traumatic for individuals and their loved ones, and any diagnosis should be delivered in person with full post-diagnosis support on offer.

☺ Never assume they know already or that someone else will have already delivered the diagnosis.

☺ However obvious it may be to you, the individual and their family may have no idea what news is coming their way.

☺ Ideal practice would involve a way of logging when a diagnosis had been delivered so health professionals can quickly check whether families are aware or not.

Hide behind medical jargon

☢ Make sure we have no idea what you're saying.

☢ Ensure that we miss all the important information.

Positive practice

☻ Lots of medical jargon is confusing and isolating for the individuals as well as their families and carers.

☻ Don't bombard them with unfamiliar terms hoping they won't then bother you with lots of questions.

☻ Always check that terms you've used are understood.

☻ And ensure that you have a good understanding of them yourself!

☻ Set the context to give them a moment to prepare themselves for what's coming – but remember Rule 1!

☻ Check that everyone concerned is really hearing you and not a 'rabbit in the headlights'.

☻ If there's limited capacity for understanding, then look to the experts in the room (family members, carers, support workers) to help with communication.

Make sure you get everything off your chest

There's no need to worry whether we've got any questions.

It doesn't matter if we're struggling to absorb the information.

Positive practice

☺ Obviously you, as the professional, have to lead the conversation, but be aware that the people in the room with you may interrupt. Make sure you hear them.

☺ This may be a speech you've given a hundred times so you may be tempted to rush through it. **Don't!** See the individual in front of you.

☺ Pause to check everyone is ok and is keeping up with the conversation.

☺ Every time will be different. Active listening will be crucial to enable you to manage the situation effectively.

☺ They may need some time to themselves to process the information they've been given and then want to ask more questions.

☺ Again, remember that this may just be another day in the office for you, but it's a potentially life-changing day for the person who is with you and that needs acknowledgement and respect.

Rule 6

Look scared and overwhelmed when delivering a diagnosis

 That way we'll know we're supposed to be scared too.

Positive practice

☺ Ask for help. As much as families need help, health professionals do too.

☺ There are several protocols to help you:

- Kaye 10 Step
- SPIKES
- ABCDE

(Information on these is given later in the booklet – see pp38-40.)

☺ Remember that a lot of communication is non-verbal so your reassurance and confidence need to be authentic.

☺ Remember that a diagnosis is useful for families, and vital if they are to get the right help and support, so it doesn't have to be scary, for you or them.

☺ Take the time to make a connection with the individuals and their families – it's reassuring and reduces fear for everyone.

Rule 7

Act dismissively when you speak to us

☢ That way we won't bother you for more information.

☢ We can see you've got other things to get on with.

Positive practice

☺ Don't rush the diagnosis and then leave. Not finding the time to do things properly makes individuals feel that they don't matter.

☺ It's essential that lines of communication are kept open to ensure holistic care.

☺ You may be used to delivering such a diagnosis, but always be mindful that it's this particular family's first and only time.

☺ Quite often it's not until they've had time to assimilate information that patients, families and carers think of more information that they need and have more questions, so make sure they have contact information for someone they can get in touch with.

☺ Make sure the individuals feel included at all times – don't make it 'everything about me, without me'.

Make sure you're sceptical of our diagnosis

☢ Just because we can make eye contact and talk doesn't mean we're not autistic.

☢ Forget that learning disabilities come in a multitude of variations.

☢ Question why we've been referred for a diagnosis, we have to fight for everything else, why not a diagnosis as well?

Positive practice

☺ Just because they don't conform to your expectations of that diagnosis doesn't mean it isn't valid.

☺ Don't dismiss the possibility of diagnosing someone or referring them for diagnosis just because they don't fit your known stereotypes.

☺ Every individual is different. Insisting they tick every box on your checklist dehumanises them.

☺ Don't dismiss their life experiences and make them doubt themselves by questioning whether they should receive a diagnosis.

☺ People with learning disabilities and on the autism spectrum deserve to be treated as individuals – see past the stereotypes to the person themselves.

☺ Use a diagnosis as a signposting tool, not as means of defining the person. Life is difficult enough - make it easier for them through listening and acceptance.

Rule 9

Assume we'll be fine now we've got our diagnosis

♣ A leaflet for a support group will be enough to send us on our way.

♣ We're not feeling at all isolated or shell-shocked...

Positive practice

☺ Families need expert advice and may be too distressed immediately after hearing the diagnosis to make any decisions about their future.

☺ Make sure that you can point people in the right direction for further information, and if you can't, then assure them you'll follow it up.

☺ Although you know the medical system and how it works, they don't. It can be confusing and distressing so they will need some pointers.

☺ Don't just send them off with a leaflet for a support group – they will need to be actively supported.

☺ Life immediately post-diagnosis can feel like looking into a void – show them small manageable steps to dealing with their new reality.

☺ Post-diagnosis support is vital for their mental well-being.

Rule 10

Assume we don't need answers if there is no diagnosis

☢ We don't need guidance, even though we've no idea where to go next.

☢ Why would we be afraid of the future, even though it's so uncertain?

☢ Even though we're going through this alone, it's not lonely at all!

Positive practice

☻ Tests in hospitals are supposed to yield results but sometimes they don't. This also needs to be handled delicately – all of the above rules still apply, but the families have to deal with a future of uncertainty, which will also require a great deal of support.

☻ **Syndromes Without A Name (SWAN UK)** https://www.undiagnosed.org.uk/ is very helpful at exploring why a diagnosis is important, how to get one, what the individual can do if you cannot give them one, and why somethings aren't diagnosable. SWAN can provide much needed support, guidance, reassurance and help at times when things can seem very dark and bleak for the individual and their family.

☻ Even without a diagnosis, GPs can put individuals on a learning disability register, which can help them get appropriate practical and financial support.

Further explanations

Rule 1: Make sure you tell us, 'I'm afraid it's bad news'

It's all too easy to allow unconsciously judgmental or emotive language to slip into conversations surrounding a diagnosis of learning disability and being on the autism spectrum. Receiving such a diagnosis should serve as a helpful tool to provide a greater sense of what the future holds, and that should not start with the implied assumption that it will be bad. It may well be a different future to the one envisaged by the individual and their loved ones, and there will no doubt be challenges, but no one gets through life without a few challenges along the way. People with learning disabilities and those on the autism spectrum deserve the opportunity to tackle their challenges with as much support and as many opportunities as others.

So, framing the language of diagnosis delivery correctly is an important first step in managing people's expectations as to what that future holds. Negative and emotive terms such as 'bad', 'I'm afraid', 'sorry', 'suffering from', are heavily loaded and that will be conveyed to the individuals and their families, burdening them with your assumptions about what life with learning disabilities and on the autism spectrum must be like. These people deserve to make up their own minds about their future, in which case they need to hear their diagnosis delivered as clearly as possible. With a thoughtless approach to framing a diagnosis, you can perpetuate the stigma that faces autistic people and those with learning disabilities throughout their life.

Instead, use this moment of diagnosis to free them of imposed, negative ideas about people with disabilities, and provide them with an opportunity to empower themselves to face the future positively. Remember, as a healthcare professional you are, in this instance, simply a conduit for information. Diagnosis delivery can still be managed in a compassionate and supportive manner without the use of loaded language.

Rule 2: Just drop that diagnosis bombshell

Again, the manner of diagnosis delivery can have a huge impact on individuals and families. It is therefore necessary to be mindful of that impact and ensure that emotional trauma from hearing a diagnosis is kept to a minimum. This entails preparation on the part of the healthcare professional delivering the diagnosis, not dropping it into the end of a conversation as an afterthought. This is a big moment for individuals to find out important information about their lives and what the future holds. Although it may be routine for you, it is definitely not routine for them – this is the first time they will have had such a diagnosis, whether or not they or their families had suspicions beforehand, and your words mark the start of their post-diagnosis life, so they need to be treated with respect.

This can be as simple as making sure there is a quiet, private space for you all to talk. If it's a daunting prospect for you then make sure you also have support, ask for help and have someone in the room with you as well.

Try to prepare them for the fact that some life-altering news is coming, but be reassuring and don't scare them – remember rule 1! If this is done in a busy corridor with lots of people coming and going it can leave families stunned and reeling. They will be anyway, so don't add to their stress. Think about how they will remember this moment. Providing a quiet, private room with space to digest information with support on standby is the least they should expect.

Rule 3: Ensure that the first we know of a diagnosis is in a letter

Having a diagnosis of any learning disability appear in a letter can be a real body blow. There's no warning that the letter contains a diagnosis, the person reading the letter is not able to ask any follow up questions or ask where to go for support, and it can leave them feeling isolated and traumatised. Diagnosis delivery should always be done face to face, whenever possible, or by phone if not, but dropped into a letter is never acceptable. Many individuals and their families have described lasting damage from the emotional trauma of first seeing a diagnosis in a letter, which quite often has been a letter about an appointment or something else entirely, with a reference to learning disabilities and being on the autism spectrum casually dropped in.

Writing a letter and using the terms 'learning disabilities' and 'autistic spectrum' is to make an assumption that they have already had the diagnosis or that the person involved and their families are aware something isn't quite as it might be. Never assume that they know already or are aware. Wherever possible, check with other health professionals involved as to whether anyone has delivered the diagnosis already, and if not, be prepared to do it yourself. Communication is key here to make sure no one slips through the cracks and receives their diagnosis in such an impersonal manner. These people need to be active participants in planning for their future, and diagnosis by letter denies them this opportunity.

Rule 4: Hide behind medical jargon

It's patronising and demeaning to hide behind complicated medical jargon. It may take some active thinking on your part as you've had years of training and practice in the medical profession, and perhaps using technical jargon and terminology comes easily to you. Some individuals with learning disabilities and those on the autism spectrum may have limited capacity for understanding the concepts and consequences of a diagnosis. Always check with them, their family members, carers or support workers and ensure they have understood that a diagnosis has been given.

Don't frighten them by making it technical and complicated – not everyone is brave enough to speak up if they haven't understood. Again, effective communication is essential to make sure everyone feels that they are part of the process and will be supported. Allow individuals and their families time to absorb the information you have given them and make sure that they are comfortable with all the terms you have used. Be prepared to spend time delivering the diagnosis in layman's terms and keep any judgmental or negative language out of the equation.

If the person uses additional communication methods then make sure you use them. Ask beforehand, either the individuals themselves or those who are with them, what the best way to communicate is and try to ensure that those methods are available on the day. It may be flagged up in the communication passport or hospital folder, so you should be able to check in advance as to the best method to deliver your diagnosis. Of course they may not yet have a communication passport or hospital folder as those resources may not be available until after diagnosis, but they may be something you can let them know about.

If in doubt, ask for help! You can ask for a learning disability nurse to be present to assist.

Rule 5: Make sure you get everything off your chest

Receiving a diagnosis is a very stressful time for people with learning disabilities and those on the autism spectrum, the impact of which cannot be underestimated. While you may feel you've had this conversation many times over, for those in the room with you now, this is their first time. They also need to be able to look back at his moment and know that it was handled with discretion and tact. It's not about making your life easier. Despite how difficult it may be as a healthcare professional to be the one delivering the diagnosis, always bear in mind how much harder it is for the people in front of you at that moment. Not harder because they won't cope with their life, but harder because they now have to deal with the stigma that their diagnosis brings. They leave your room knowing that they now have to adapt everything they do to try and live a successful and fulfilling life in a society entirely biased towards those who don't share their diagnosis.

So don't rush through your news. You need to be engaged and actively observing how the news is being received. Give them space and an opportunity to ask questions as you go along. Don't just deliver your piece and leave. Individuals should always feel able to interrupt and ask questions. Hospitals and other healthcare settings can feel very intimidating to those accessing their services so the onus is on you to ensure they are not intimidated. Watch out for that 'rabbit in the headlights' look and offer emotional and practical support as necessary.

Rule 6: Look scared and overwhelmed when delivering a diagnosis

There are support structures in place if you are feeling overwhelmed with the prospect of delivering a diagnosis. The following steps are taken from the Royal College of Nursing's guidelines on delivering diagnoses in general. Unfortunately they include the term 'bad news', which we are trying to steer away from, but the advice itself can help manage the situation and smooth the way for everyone involved:

SPIKES: a six-step protocol for breaking bad news:

Step 1 – SETTING up the interview

Step 2 – Assessing the patient's (parent's) PERCEPTION

Step 3 – Obtaining the patient's (parent's) INVITATION

Step 4 – Giving KNOWLEDGE and information

Step 5 – Addressing the patient's (parent's) EMOTIONS with empathy

Step 6 – STRATEGY and summary

(Modified from Baile W, Buckman R, Lenzi R, Glober G, Beale E and Kudleka A (2000) SPIKES – a six step protocol for delivering bad news: application to the patient with cancer. *Oncologist* **5** pp302-311)

The ABCDE mnemonic for breaking bad news:

Advance preparation

Build a therapeutic environment/relationship

Communicate well

Deal with patient and family reactions

Encourage and validate emotions

(Adapted from Rabow MW and McPhee SJ (1999) Beyond breaking bad news: how to help patients who suffer. *Western Journal of Medicine* **171** pp260-263)

Kaye's 10 step model:

Step 1: Preparation

Step 2: What does the patient (parent) know?

Step 3: Is more information wanted?

Step 4: Give a warning shot

Step 5: Allow denial

Step 6: Explain if requested

Step 7: Listen to concerns

Step 8: Encourage ventilation of feelings

Step 9: Summarise

Step 10: Offer further help

(Modified from Kaye P (1996) *Breaking bad news: a 10 step approach,* Northampton: EPL)

Be aware that many people with learning disabilities pick up on body language and non-verbal clues, so even though you may think you're doing fine, you may inadvertently be communicating stress and fear. Looking down at medical notes all the time, shuffling through papers and avoiding eye contact can make people nervous and worried.

On the other hand, some people on the autism spectrum may be unable to interpret body language or facial expressions and will rely on exact, functional language without any opportunity for misinterpretation to fully grasp what they're being told.

Rule 7: Act dismissively when you speak to us

All too often a diagnosis is delivered by someone who has been through the process a hundred times before and has got a lot of other things going on. It's therefore important to remember that, for the individual concerned and their loved ones, this is a life-changing moment and a dismissive or hurried approach by you can be devastating. It can make them feel as though their journey is of no importance and they do not feel empowered to ask questions or seek guidance. It also suggests to the individuals and their families that you are more important than them – you're too busy and need to get this out of the way as soon as possible. Always take time and prepare properly when you are about to deliver a diagnosis.

People with learning disabilities and those on the autism spectrum need to be treated with dignity and humanity; don't write them off just because you've done your bit. And never destroy their hope. Just because they may now be on a different path to the one they thought they were on, and a different one to yours, doesn't mean it's the wrong path. It's their path and they need the way well signposted and well lit.

Actively engaging with them can go some way to ensuring they feel as though they are being treated like human beings, not just on the production line in some giant health care factory.

Rule 8: Make sure you're sceptical of our diagnosis

Every single human being on the planet is an individual, possessing their own unique personality traits, talents, likes and dislikes. And that includes people with learning disabilities and those on the autism spectrum. They have as much right to be treated with dignity as anyone else. This means seeing beyond the diagnosis you may be about to deliver to the person themselves. Don't make assumptions about someone just based on what you think you know about learning disabilities and being on the autism spectrum.

You are seeing them at a moment in time on their life journey. Perhaps they are able to mask elements of their disabilities or condition. Perhaps they're having a really good day and their disabilities may not be immediately obvious to you, which may leave you wondering how they managed to get a referral. Be aware that most of their life will have been a battle for them and a diagnosis can bring clarity and understanding as well as practical support. It's that 'Ah! That explains a lot!' moment, when they can go from doubting themselves to reassuring themselves. Make sure you are part of the reassuring process here, not the doubting. Many people are not diagnosed, particularly with ASD, until later in life because they haven't shown the 'correct' attributes to be given that diagnosis. It's possible you genuinely don't believe that a diagnosis is necessary, but make sure the individual doesn't leave their appointment with you still searching for answers, only to find them years later and wonder how different life would have been had they received the diagnosis earlier.

Conforming to established expectations of how certain conditions manifest themselves is an added burden for anyone with intellectual disabilities and on the autism spectrum. Support and an open mind from healthcare professionals can go a long way to getting the right practical, financial and emotional support in place.

Rule 9: Assume we'll be fine now we've got our diagnosis

Delivering a diagnosis is not where your responsibilities end. It's incredibly isolating for families to feel as though they're on their own as soon as they've received a diagnosis of learning disability or being on the autism spectrum. They will not necessarily have any perspective on the condition or know where to go for help.

Being handed a leaflet for a support group and being ushered out the door is not enough. Quite often people don't feel emotionally strong enough to get themselves to a support group, and so their isolation grows, leading to additional issues.

The internet can be a wonderful tool for finding out additional information, but it can also lead to misunderstandings and it does not make up for human contact and guidance. If you are not able to offer post-diagnosis support, find someone who can. Make a plan with the family so that they leave the room feeling supported and knowing where to turn next, and have someone they can contact if they have more questions.

Rule 10: Assume we don't need answers if there is no diagnosis

While every individual is more than just a diagnosis, having no diagnosis at all can be just as devastating as receiving one. The anticipation of every appointment, hoping that answers will finally be forthcoming only to be let down every time as there are no definitive answers can be very emotionally draining and a real struggle for people trying to get a handle on what their or their loved ones' future might look like. What a family may have thought was a medical issue that could be cured, for example with medication, suddenly begins to look more and more like a life-long condition, and, with no diagnosis, adjustment periods can take years.

For many families, acquiring a diagnosis remains very important as their child grows up. Not having one means they can struggle to access the right care and support. They may have no concept of what the future has in store for their child or if other children they were planning on having might be similarly affected.

Although parents tend to know that having a diagnosis is unlikely to significantly alter their child's life, they often hope it will provide them with a greater sense of what is to come.

People without a diagnosis need a lot of support and reassurance as they will be feeling very isolated. They will have a lot of questions: how can I get appropriate support? If we have more children will they also have learning disabilities? What's going to happen in the future? Will they be well? Will they survive? You can steer them to support groups such as SWAN[1], who can help explore why a diagnosis is important, how to get one, what to do if you cannot get one and why some things aren't diagnosable. SWAN can provide much needed support, guidance, reassurance and help.

---

1 Syndromes Without A Name (SWAN UK) https://www.undiagnosed.org.uk/

A family's story: In the beginning, the fight

'In the early days I fought against the system, I fought against the fact that suddenly your life was not your own, that even 18-year-old student nurses could sit and read notes about your child that you were not allowed to look at. Lives on view for all to see, every emotion, every outburst.

'The first lesson I learnt was that when your child is really complicated and has a really rare condition then medicine becomes no more than educated guesswork. The doctors don't have all the answers, the ones you respect are the ones who will admit that they don't know what to do and will work with you to find out.

'The internet becomes your best friend and your enemy. You spend hours trawling through case studies, trying to find the answer that will help your child. Believe me, as time goes by you don't go to the internet anymore. It does not have all the answers; your child is unique and while the internet will give you pointers there are no guarantees that treatments that work for others will work for your child. You do not have to be alone. It took me a long time to realise that. And

by talking and opening up to other parents who have walked your path you can gain the benefit of their experience, what they did that worked, what they wished they had done.

'I have learned time and time again that it is important to have a good relationship with the doctors treating your child. You don't have to like them, but you have to work with them. I have learned over the years that doctors really do care, even the ones that appear not to, some of them don't have the best bedside manner; some are very arrogant. Yes, they can go home and switch off, but they all have your child's best interests at heart and sometimes their views will clash with yours.

'This is why taking another person along to meetings, involving a support group, an intermediary, the PALs [patient advice and liaison] service is so important, because at the time in your life when you are dealing with the most extreme of emotions and are so terrified that you may lose your child, you also have to be calm, rational and efficient.'

Stephanie Nimmo

References

Blair J, Busk M, Goleniowska H, Hawtrey-Woore S, Morris S, Newbold Y & Nimmo S (2016) Through our eyes: What parents want for their children from health professionals. In: S Hardy, E Chaplin and P Woodward (2016) *Supporting the Physical Health Needs of People with Learning Disabilities: A handbook for professionals, support staff and families*. Brighton: Pavilion Publishing.

Blair J (2013) Everybody's life has worth: getting it right in hospital for people with an intellectual disability and reducing clinical risks. *Clinical Risk* **19** 58–63.

Hollins S & Hollins M (2005) *You and Your Child: Making sense of learning disabilities*. London: Karnac Books.

Newbold Y (2014) *The Special Parent's Handbook*. Poole: Amity Books.

Royal College of Nursing (2013) *Breaking Bad News: Supporting parents when they are told of their child's diagnosis*.

Turk J (2014) Developmental disabilities: Labelling and definitions. *The Bridge (The Association for Child and Adolescent Mental Health) Issue 01*

Useful websites and resources

British Institute of Learning Disabilities (BILD)
www.bild.org.uk
The institute helps develop the organisations that provide services and the people who give support.

Books Beyond Words
www.booksbeyondwords.co.uk
Publishes accessible stories in pictures to help people with learning and communication disabilities explore and understand their own experiences.

Disability Matters
www.disabilitymatters.org.uk
An e-learning resource to enhance understanding and skills of staff.

Down's Side Up
www.downsideup.com
Gently changing perceptions of Down's syndrome.

Easyhealth
www.easyhealth.org.uk
Provides over 250 free accessible leaflets, health guides and videos.

Mencap
http://www.bacdis.org.uk/policy/documents/
Gettingitright.pdf
A group of organisations working towards better
healthcare, well-being and quality of life for people
with a learning disability.

**NHS Choices, Going into Hospital with
a Learning Disability**
http://www.nhs.uk/Livewell/Childrenwithalearning
disability/Pages/Going-into-hospital-withlearning
disability.aspx
Information on preparing a person with a learning
disability for hospital.

Syndromes Without A Name SWAN UK
https://www.undiagnosed.org.uk/

University of Hertfordshire
http://www.intellectualdisability.info/Understanding

Useful training and development resources from Pavilion Publishing

Pavilion Publishing (www.pavpub.com) publishes a range of resources for staff working in learning disability and autism, here are some of the range of products they have available.

Successful Health Screening through Desensitisation for People with Learning Disabilities: A training and resource pack for healthcare professionals

By Lisa Harrington and Sarah Walker

Supporting the Physical Health Needs of People with Learning Disabilities: A handbook for professionals, support staff and families

Edited by Steve Hardy, Eddie Chaplin and Peter Woodward

Taking Control of My Health: A training manual for health and social care staff to deliver a course for people with learning disabilities who have health conditions

By Mary Codling

Supporting Women with Learning Disabilities through the Menopause: A manual and training resource for health and social care workers

By Michelle McCarthy and Lorraine Millard

Understanding Emotions in People with Learning Disabilities: Factsheets to help staff understand and manage emotions of sadness, anxiety and anger in people with learning disabilities

By Surrey and Borders Partnership NHS Foundation Trust

A Mismatch of Salience: Explorations of the nature of autism from theory to practice

The collected writings of Dr Damian Milton.

Ten Rules for Ensuring People with Learning Disabilities and Those Who Are On the Autism Spectrum Develop Challenging Behaviour... and maybe what to do about it

By Damian Milton and Richard Mills with Simon Jones

Ten Rules for Ensuring People with Learning Disabilities Can't Access Healthcare... and maybe what to do about it

By Viki Ainsworth and Jim Blair

Autism and Intellectual Disability in Adults, Volumes 1 and 2

Edited by Dr Damian Milton and Professor Nicola Martin

Understanding and Supporting Children and Adults on the Autism Spectrum: A training and learning resource

By Julie Beadle-Brown and Richard Mills